Do You Know The One?

LISTEN TO THE BOOK "DO YOU KNOW THE ONE?"
Narrated by: John Bentley
Music by: Asha Imuno & Noah Bentley

MICHELLE BENTLEY

Illustrated by LOUISE HARGREAVES

Copyright © 2022 Michelle Bentley.

All rights reserved. No part of this book may be used or reproduced by any means, graphic, electronic, or mechanical, including photocopying, recording, taping or by any information storage retrieval system without the written permission of the author except in the case of brief quotations embodied in critical articles and reviews.

WestBow Press books may be ordered through booksellers or by contacting:

WestBow Press
A Division of Thomas Nelson & Zondervan
1663 Liberty Drive
Bloomington, IN 47403
www.westbowpress.com
844-714-3454

Because of the dynamic nature of the Internet, any web addresses or links contained in this book may have changed since publication and may no longer be valid. The views expressed in this work are solely those of the author and do not necessarily reflect the views of the publisher, and the publisher hereby disclaims any responsibility for them.

Any people depicted in stock imagery provided by Getty Images are models, and such images are being used for illustrative purposes only.
Certain stock imagery © Getty Images.

Interior Image Credit: Louise Hargreaves

Scriptures taken from the Holy Bible, New International Version®, NIV®. Copyright © 1973, 1978, 1984, 2011 by Biblica, Inc.™ Used by permission of Zondervan. All rights reserved worldwide. www.zondervan.com The "NIV" and "New International Version" are trademarks registered in the United States Patent and Trademark Office by Biblica, Inc.®

ISBN: 978-1-6642-5408-4 (sc)
ISBN: 978-1-6642-5410-7 (hc)
ISBN: 978-1-6642-5409-1 (e)

Library of Congress Control Number: 2021925734

Printed in the United States of America.

WestBow Press rev. date: 3/29/2022

My prayer for this book is that it would help little ones understand and know the Creator of this wonderful world …

That it would plant seeds of Biblical truth in every heart, from the youngest to the oldest …

And that we would always be joyfully overwhelmed by the splendor of God's great creation.

To my grown boys, Jentrie, Noah, Maxwell and Quincy, I love you with all my heart! I cheerfully dedicate this book to you, your children, and to your children's children.

May you always know and love the One who created the whole wide world and everything in it!
- love Mom

To my husband John, you are my number one supporter and have loved me and this book from the start!

Do you know the one... who created the whole wide world?

Come along, my friend, and you will see.

He did it to light the night, form time, and fill space. Genesis 1:16-18

Love Peace

Do you know the one... who created the brilliant Sun and the bright Moon?

He did it to light up our mornings

and our late afternoons.

Genesis 1:14–15

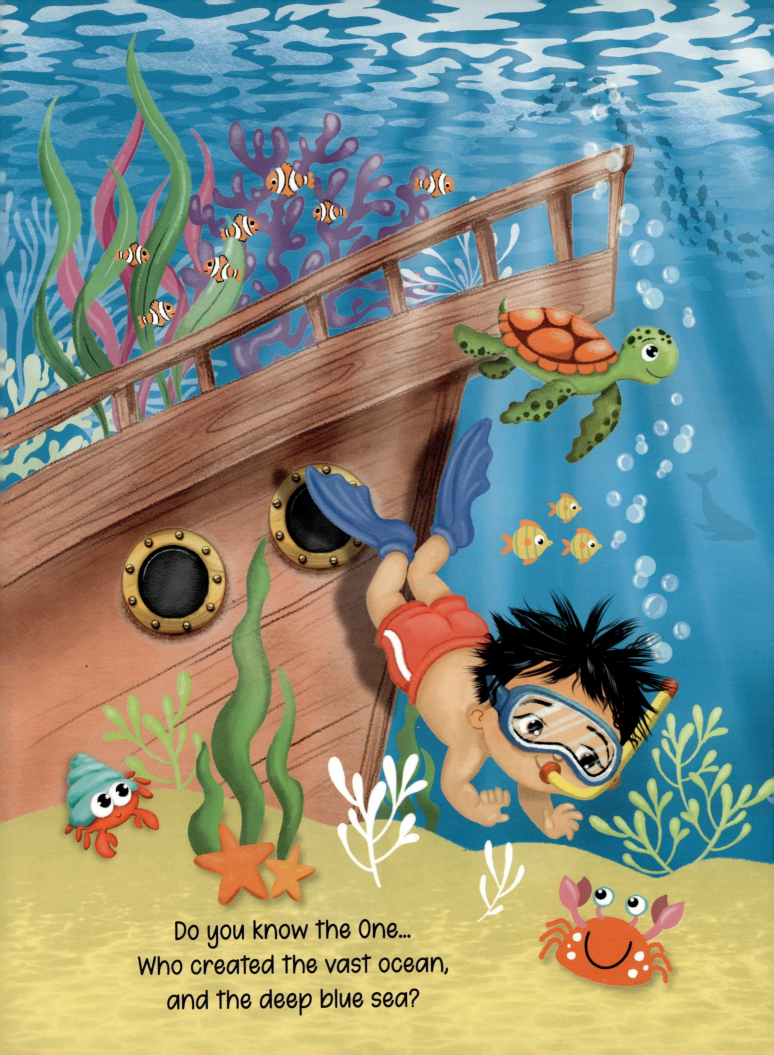

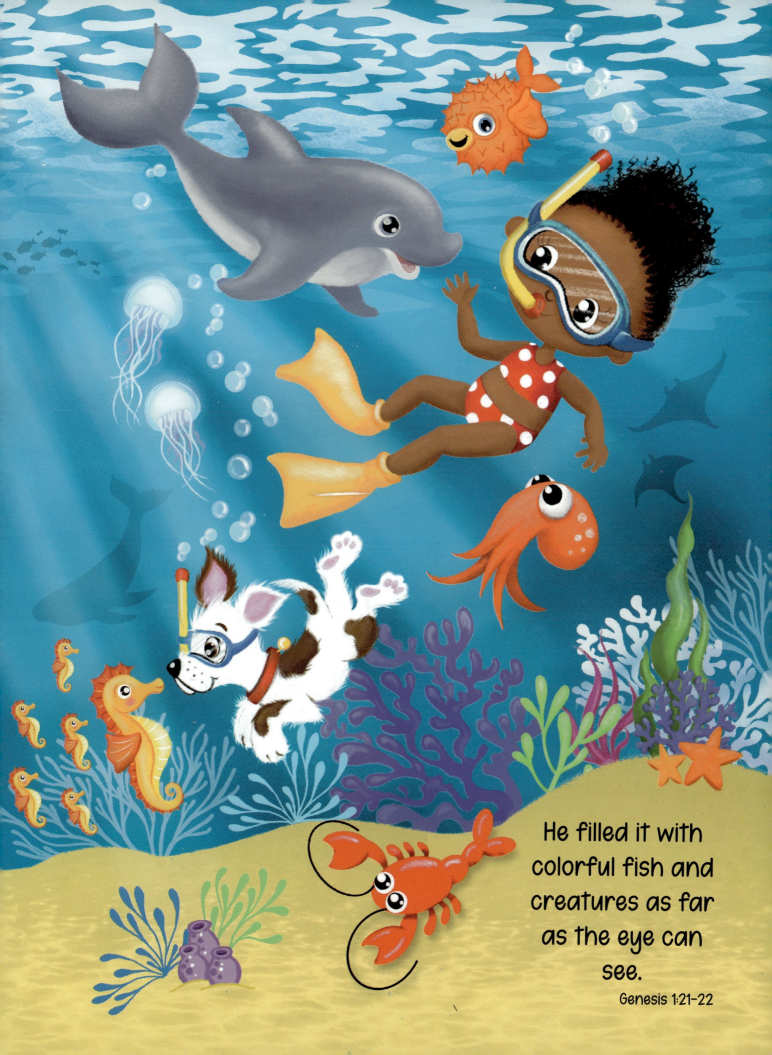

Do you know the One...
Who shaped the mighty mountains that we climb?

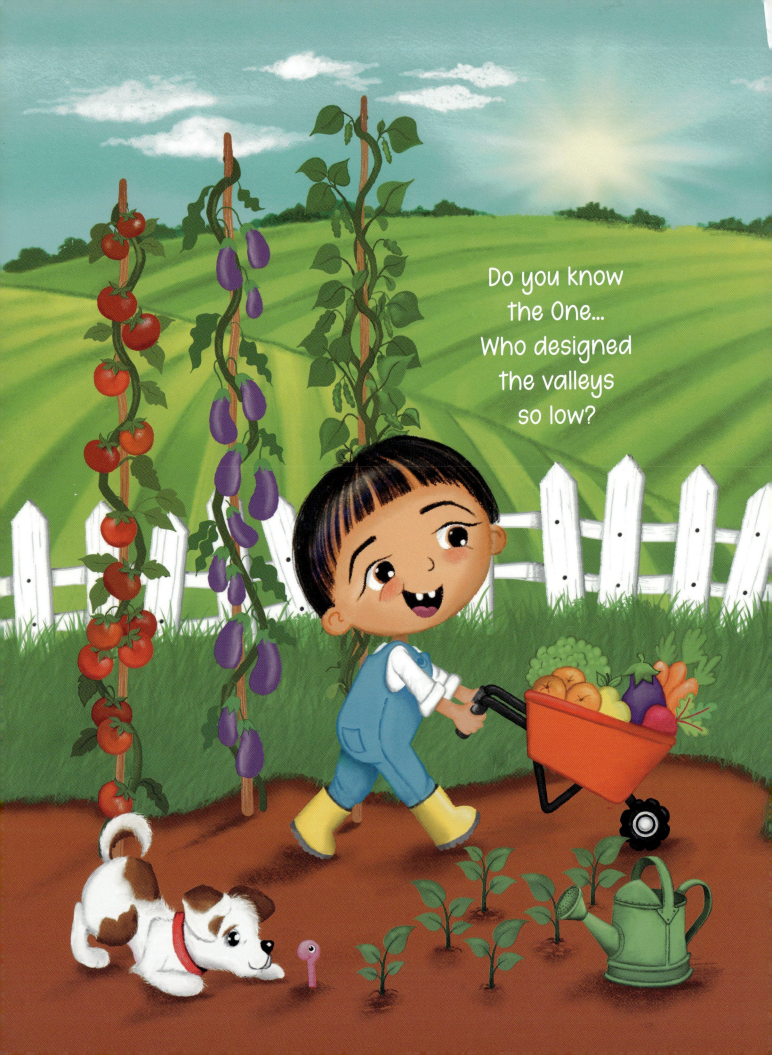

He made this a perfect place for fruits and veggies to grow.

Genesis 1:11–12

Do you know the One... Who created the animals, both big and small?

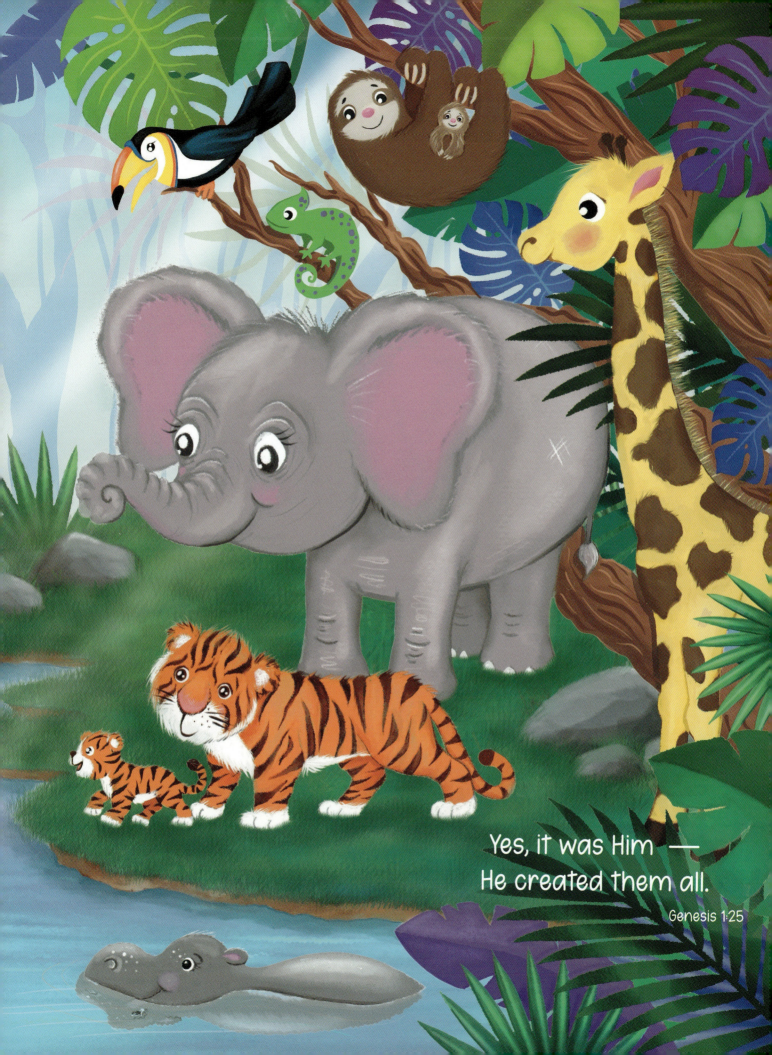

Do you know the One...

Who made all the people of all the lands?

He can hold every one of us in the palm of His hand.

Isaiah 41:13

Do you know the One...

Who made the young, the old,
the short, and the tall?

Place your
child's photo
here

We are His most favorite
masterpiece of all.

Ephesians 2:10

Do you know the One?
Have you figured it out?

Scripture References

And God said, "Let there be lights in the expanse of the heavens to separate the day from the night. And let them be signs and for seasons, and for days and years, and let them be lights in the expanse of the heavens to give light upon the earth." And it was so. Genesis 1:14-15

And God made the two great lights – the greater light to rule the day and lesser light to rule the night – and the stars. And God set them in the expanse of the heavens to give lights on the earth, to rule over the day and over the night, and to separate the light from the darkness. And God saw that it was good. And there was evening and there was morning, the fourth day. Genesis 1: 16-19

So God created the great sea creatures and every living creature that moves, with which the waters swarm, according to their kinds, and every winged bird according to its kind. And God saw that it was good. And God blessed them, saying, "Be fruitful and multiply and fill the waters in the seas, and let birds multiply on the earth." Genesis 1:21-22

For behold, he who forms the mountains and creates the wind, and declares to man what is his thought, who makes the morning, darkness, and treads on the heights of the earth – the Lord, the God of hosts is his name! Amos 4:13

And God said, "Let the earth sprout vegetation, plants yielding seed, and fruit trees bearing fruit in which is their seed, each according to its kind, on the earth." And it was so. The earth brought forth vegetation, plants yielding seed, according to their own kinds, and trees bearing fruit in which is their seed, each according to its kind. And God saw that it was good. Genesis 1:11-12

And God made the beasts of the earth according to their kinds and the livestock according to their kinds, and everything that creeps on the ground according to its kind, And God saw that it was good. Genesis 1:25

And God said, "This is the sign of the covenant that I make between me and you and every living creature that is with you, for all future generations: I have set my bow in the cloud, and it shall be a sign of the covenant between me and the earth." Genesis 9:12-13

"For I hold you by your right hand – I, the Lord your God. And I say to you, "Don't be afraid, I am here to you help you." Isaiah 41:13

"For we are God's masterpiece. He has created us anew in Christ Jesus, so we can do the good things, He planned for us long ago." Ephesians 2:10

In the beginning God created the heavens and the earth. Now the earth was formless and empty, darkness was over the surface of the deep, and the Spirit of God was hovering over the waters. Genesis 1:1-2

ABOUT THE AUTHOR

MICHELLE BENTLEY, is a wife and mother of four young men. She has served in ministries impacting women, families and children for over two decades. Michelle has a heart for women ministries and is the founder of Spiritual Refreshing and Simply Gathering.

She raised her boys on adventurous stories, and has a deep appreciation for beautifully illustrated children's books. It is her desire that, Do you know the One would reach readers both young and old to help make known the Creator of this remarkable world.

ABOUT THE ILLUSTRATOR

Louise Hargreaves is an Illustrator from England. After graduating from Liverpool Art School, Louise worked in the greetings card industry before making the leap to become a freelance artist.

She loves to travel, and lived and worked in Australia for a number of years. She now lives in a little village in Yorkshire, England with her family. She loves sitting down to draw with a hot cup of tea, taking long walks in the countryside, and spending time with her family.